D1561226

EMC132-The Civil War (eBook)

Mason Crest Publishers 5 Volumes Flipbook
Set Price: $183.00
Reading Level: 7th Grade, 8th Grade, Young Adult
Interest Level: Secondary
Accelerated Reader: No

Here the roots of the conflict are examined from the political situation before the war to the decision made to wage war on fellow citizens. The Civil War would prove to be the ultimate test for the soldiers who fought and for their country.

Title	Code	List Price	Our Price	Copyright	Prg
Civil War Victory and the Costly Aftermath	EMC278963	$36.60	$36.60	2018	
Slavery and the Abolition Movement	EMC278932	$36.60	$36.60	2018	
The Battle of Gettysburg – The Turning Point in the Civil War	EMC278949	$36.60	$36.60	2018	
The Origins of the Civil War	EMC278925	$36.60	$36.60	2018	
The Politics of the Civil War	EMC278956	$36.60	$36.60	2018	

THE ORIGINS OF THE CIVIL WAR

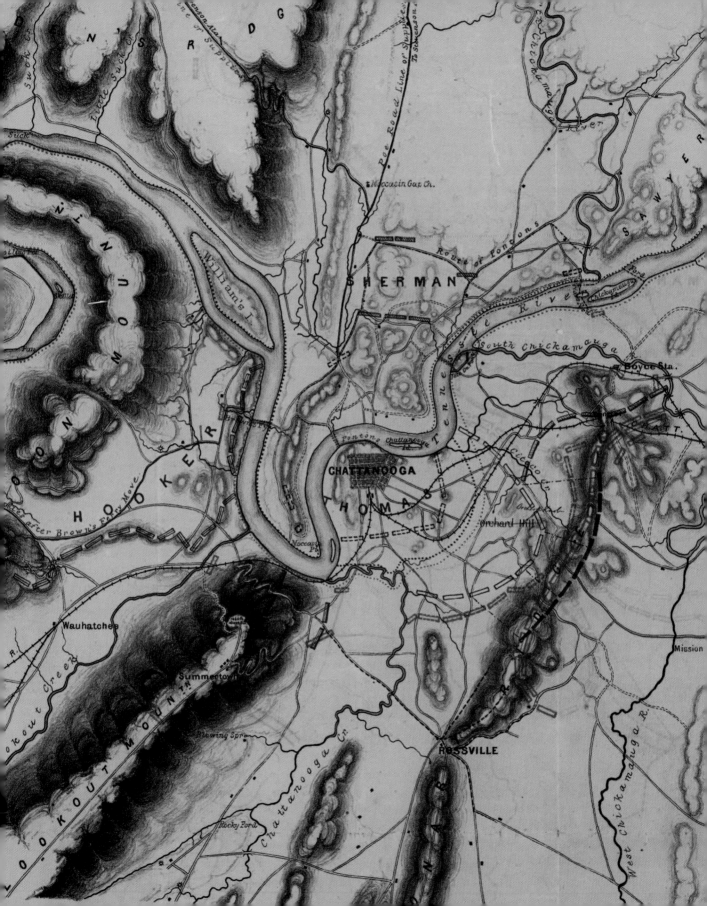

THE ORIGINS OF THE CIVIL WAR

Jonathan Sutherland & Diane Canwell

MASON CREST

Mason Crest
450 Parkway Drive, Suite D
Broomall, PA 19008
www.masoncrest.com

© 2018 by Mason Crest, an imprint of National Highlights, Inc.

All rights reserved. No part of this publication may be reproduced
or transmitted in any form or by any means, electronic or mechanical,
including photocopying, recording, taping, or any information storage
and retrieval system, without permission in writing from the
copyright holder.

Cataloging-in-Publication Data on file with the Library of Congress.

Printed and bound in the United States of America.

First printing
9 8 7 6 5 4 3 2 1

ISBN: 978-1-4222-3882-0
Series ISBN: 978-1-4222-3881-3
ebook ISBN: 978-1-4222-7892-5
ebook series ISBN: 978-1-4222-7891-8

Produced by Regency House Publishing Limited
The Manor House
High Street
Buntingford
Hertfordshire
SG9 9AB
United Kingdom

www.regencyhousepublishing.com

Text copyright © 2018 Regency House Publishing Limited/Jonathan Sutherland and
Diane Canwell.

PAGE 2: Sketch of the Battle of
Chattanooga. November 23–26, 1863.

PAGE 3: Brandy Station, Virginia.
Officers' winter headquarters. Army of the
Potomac Date: ca. 1864.

RIGHT: Ruins of a paper mill at
Richmond, Virginia.

PAGE 6: Gettysburg Battlefield site.

CONTENTS

KEY ICONS TO LOOK FOR:

 Words to Understand: These words with their easy-to-understand definitions will increase the reader's understanding of the text, while building vocabulary skills.

 Sidebars: This boxed material within the main text allows readers to build knowledge, gain insights, explore possibilities, and broaden their perspectives by weaving together additional information to provide realistic and holistic perspectives.

 Educational Videos: Readers can view videos by scanning our QR codes, providing them with additional content to supplement the text. Examples include news coverage, moments in history, speeches, iconic sports moments, and much more!

 Text-Dependent Questions: These questions send the reader back to the text for more careful attention to the evidence presented here.

 Research Projects: Readers are pointed toward areas of further inquiry connected to each chapter. Suggestions are provided for projects that encourage deeper research and analysis.

 Series Glossary of Key Terms: This back-of-the-book glossary contains terminology used throughout the series. Words found here increase the reader's ability to read and comprehend high-level books and articles in this field.

OPPOSITE: Tomb of unknown Civil War soliders at Arlington National Cemetery, Virginia.

QUIET
RESPECT
PLEASE

Lincoln Memorial

The grand Lincoln Memorial is an American national monument built to honor the 16th President of the United States, Abraham Lincoln. It was designed by Henry Bacon, a New York architect. He had spent time studying in Europe where he was influenced and inspired by ancient Greek architecture. It was based on the architecture of a Greek temple. There are 36 Doric columns, each one representing one state of the U.S. at the date of President Lincoln's death.

The memorial contains a large seated sculpture of Abraham Lincoln. The nineteen-foot tall statue of Abraham Lincoln was designed by Daniel Chester French who was a leading sculptor from Massachusetts. The marble statue was carved in white Georgia marble by the Piccirilli brothers. The interior murals were painted by Jules Guerin. Ernest C. Bairstow created the exterior details with carvings by Evelyn Beatrice Longman. The memorial is inscribed with Lincoln's famous speech, "The Gettysburg Address." The words of the speech are etched into the wall to inspire all Americans just as it did in 1863. To the right is the entire Second Inaugural Address, given by Lincoln in March 1865. The memorial itself is 190 feet long, 119 feet wide, and almost 100 feet high. It took 8 years to complete from 1914–1922.

At its most basic level the Lincoln Memorial symbolizes the idea of Freedom. The Lincoln Memorial is often used as a gathering place for protests and political rallies. The Memorial has become a symbolically sacred venue especially for the Civil Rights movement. On August 28, 1963, the memorial grounds were the site of the *March on Washington for Jobs and Freedom*, which proved to the high point of the *American Civil Rights Movement*. It is estimated that approximately 250,000 people came to the event, where they heard Martin Luther King, Jr. deliver his historic speech *"I have a Dream."* King's speech, with its language of patriotism and its evocation of Lincoln's Gettysburg Address, was meant to match the symbolism of the Lincoln Memorial as a monument to national unity.

The Lincoln Memorial is located on the western end of the National Mall in Washington, D.C., across from the Washington Monument, and towers over the Reflecting Pool. The memorial is maintained by the U.S. National Park Service, and receives approximately 8 million visitors each year. It is open 24 hours a day and is free to all visitors.

The Battle of Shiloh.
Chromolithograph by Thulstrup D. Thure, 1888.

Chapter One
THE BEGINNINGS OF THE CONFLICT

For many years after the American Civil War (1861–1865), Northerners would refer to it as the War of the Rebellion. It had been the second conflict in less than a century, the first, the American **Revolution** (the War of American Independence), having resulted in the Declaration of Independence in 1776 and the expulsion of the British. Many saw the conflict as something more than a popular uprising against an occupying force, regarding it as an event of far-

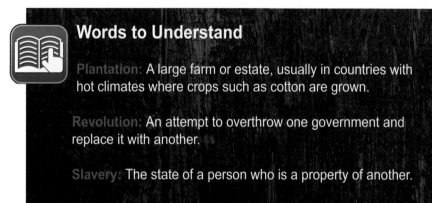

Words to Understand

Plantation: A large farm or estate, usually in countries with hot climates where crops such as cotton are grown.

Revolution: An attempt to overthrow one government and replace it with another.

Slavery: The state of a person who is a property of another.

OPPOSITE: Dependent on the labor of slaves, who represented the great majority of the American black population, the great Southern plantations were both homes and sources of income for a white elite.

ABOVE: A trader in slaves, in Alexandria, Virginia.

reaching consequence to America and to the world at large. On that occasion, Europe had played a direct role; the British on the one hand, supported by loyalists against the insurgents and their allies, and on the other, America, supported by France and Spain.

Contrary to popular belief, the American Civil War, initially at least, did not arise out of the slave question – its roots lay deeper than that.

Southern historians called it "the war between the states," in that the South saw it as a consequence of the North's resistance to its right to withdraw from the Union, each state seeing itself as sovereign though in confederation with its neighbors.

This was not the first time the Union had been under threat; since 1820 the South had become more and more alarmed by developments within

LEFT: Assault on Fort Sanders.
Union troops led by General Burnside fighting Confederates led by General Longstreet. November 29, 1863.

the United States. The North had grown more populous and wealthy, its economy based not on agriculture but on proliferating industry. The South began to see its power slipping away, and its position within the Union beginning to erode. With their distinctive identity and shared past, the Southern states began to see the inevitability of an independent future.

While the Old South did have a distinctive identity of its own, it was not, as many imagined, a huge cotton **plantation** teeming with slaves controlled by overseers. Slavery was not only endemic in the South, it was

ABOVE: The pens where the slaves were kept while they waited to be sold.

OPPOSITE : Abraham Lincoln. Lithograph by John H. Bufford, Bufford's Publishing House, ca.1862.

LEFT: Preparing cotton for the gin on Smith's plantation, Port Royal Island, South Carolina. *Photograph by Timothy O'Sullivan, ca. 1862.*

ULYSSES S. GRANT (1822–1885)

Grant was born at Point Pleasant, Ohio. He was not considered to be particularly bright academically, but he entered West Point in 1839. This is where he discovered his name had been registered incorrectly and at that point dropped Hiram as a Christian name. He graduated twenty-first out of thirty-nine in 1843 and served with distinction during the Mexican War, where he was associated with Zachary Taylor and Winfield Scott. Grant resigned his commission in 1854 and worked as a clerk in his father's business, where there were rumors of heavy drinking and poor discipline. In May 1861 he was given command of a regiment of infantry, but by August he was a brigadier general. He earned his nickname, "Unconditional Surrender" Grant, in February 1862, when he demanded the surrender of trapped Confederate troops. He was in command of the army by April 1862 and fought the bloodiest battle of the war at Shiloh. Grant was given command of the Department of Tennessee in October 1862 and launched his assaults on Vicksburg. He took the city and was promoted to major general and subsequently fought the Battles of Chickamauga, Chattanooga, Lookout Mountain, and Missionary Ridge. Soon after he was promoted to lieutenant general and now commanded all Union armies. He accompanied Meade to fight the Wilderness Campaign, Spotsylvania and Cold Harbor, where casualties earned him the new nickname of "Butcher Grant." In June 1864 he attached himself to the Army of the Potomac, remaining with it until April 1865. Sheridan's victory at Five Forks on April 1, 1865 forced Lee to abandon Richmond and Petersburg and Grant was there to cut off Lee's retreat. It was by mutual agreement that the Army of Northern Virginia finally surrendered to Grant at Appomattox Courthouse. After the war Grant became a full general in 1866, and two years later stood as Republican candidate for president and won. He surrounded himself with friends and was not considered to be a successful president, but was nevertheless re-elected in 1872. He left office in 1877 and traveled around the world for two years, returning home short of money. He was forced to sell off his wartime memorabilia and was declared bankrupt in 1884. By now, he was suffering from throat cancer: he died in July 1885 in New York and his remains lie in a mausoleum in the city.

also a blight on the lives of the slaves themselves, and a time bomb ready to explode. While the black population of the North was insignificant, in the South it outnumbered its white masters by more than half.

Even as the influence of the South began to wane, tariffs failed to lighten the burden on Southern agriculture. At every turn, Federal policies seemed to favor the North: the South produced vast wealth for the Union, but received very little in return. These grievances were similar to those heard in the 13 colonies in the American Revolution, when "no taxation without representation" was the call. The South was beginning to perceive itself as little more than an exploited colony.

South Carolina threatened to secede from the Union as early as 1832, at about the same time as militant abolitionists were beginning to gather strength in the North. The abolitionists claimed slavery to be in direct contradiction to the Declaration of Independence in which all men were to be considered equal. In short, the militants believed that slavery and democracy were totally incompatible with one another.

Ten years earlier, **slavery** had not featured largely in national debates, but with the Mexican War over and huge new territories opening up for settlement, the question of slavery was now very much on the agenda. A compromise was made in 1850, which called only a temporary halt to the debate and the inevitable conflict that would ensue.

The two key issues that would propel the United States into war had not been resolved, despite nearly 50 years of negotiations. First was the issue of secession – the right of a state to leave the Union if it so wished. The second was the unresolved question of extending slavery into the new territories. In fact, the spark that would ignite the conflict was the election of Abraham Lincoln in November 1860, and his implacable opposition to the extension of slavery into the new territories.

Extremists on both sides were unwilling to compromise on either issue, and peaceful resolution was now impossible. It would be South Carolina, which had threatened secession 30 years earlier, that would force the issue. On December 20, 1860, at a convention in Charleston, the state adopted an Ordnance of Secession. It repealed its 1788 ratification of the Constitution and proclaimed the new act effective from December 24, 1860.

RIGHT: The Shackle Broken ...
Lithograph illustrating Robert B. Elliott's famous speech in favor of the Civil Rights Act, delivered by the House of Representatives in 1874.

OVERLEAF: Enslaved African-Americans running from Hampton, Virginia to Fort Monroe seeking sanctuary from slavery in August 1861.
19th century engraving.

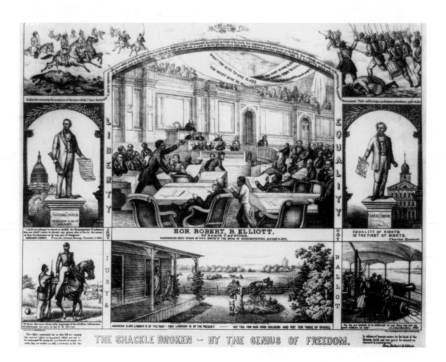

ABOVE: Emancipation
Thomas Nast (1840–1902).
Thomas Nast's celebration of the emancipation of Southern slaves with the end of the Civil War, 1865.
Engraving. Published by S. Bott, Philadelphia, Pennsylvania.

RIGHT: A Black soldier.

Text-Dependent Questions

1. How long did the American Civil War last for?

2. What year was the Declaration of Independence?

3. When was Abraham Lincoln elected as president?

ABOVE: Gabions used in the fortification of Fort Sumter, Charleston, South Carolina, during seaborne expeditions against the Atlantic coast of the Confederacy during the Civil War.

RIGHT: Fugitives fording the Rappahannock river in the summer of 1862. The slaves took advantage of the Second Battle of Bull Run to escape to Union lines.

Research Project

For many years after the American Civil War (1861–1865), Northerners would refer to it as the War of the Rebellion. Explain why Northerners gave it this term?

Chapter Two
THE WAR BREAKS OUT

Hostilities did not begin until the following April: on April 12, 1861 rebel forces opened fire on the Federal-held Fort Sumter in Charleston harbor. The war would officially last for just over four years.

As North and South divided and plunged into war, comrades-in-arms who had known one another from their days at the U.S. Military Academy at West Point went their

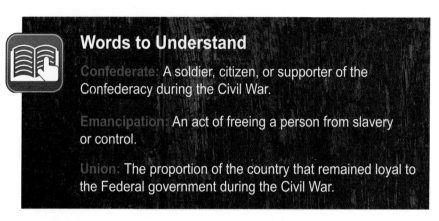

Words to Understand

Confederate: A soldier, citizen, or supporter of the Confederacy during the Civil War.

Emancipation: An act of freeing a person from slavery or control.

Union: The proportion of the country that remained loyal to the Federal government during the Civil War.

ABOVE: Thomas "Stonewall" Jackson.

RIGHT: Philip H. Sheridan.

separate ways. For both officers and rank and file alike, the simple choice was to rally to the flag of their state, regardless of their views of the political situation. Others aligned themselves to their chosen political or philosophical belief, much to the disgust of their families: the American Civil War, like all internal conflicts, truly pitted brother against brother.

In a war that would see massed muskets and terrifying artillery bombardment, casualties were bound to be high. A dense line of men firing at one another at a ruinous distance was a test of nerve. As men fell up and down the line, depleting the firepower and resolve of the regiment, officers put themselves at extreme risk to convince their men to stand firm. Regimental and company officers had only a 15 percent chance of being killed or wounded, while brigade, divisional, and corps commanders were 50 percent more likely to be hit – simply because they were expected to lead from the front.

The key military figures of the American Civil War were drawn from the tiny pre-war standing army. These men, the majority of whom had passed through West Point, had cut their teeth in earlier clashes, either against the Mexicans or against Native Americans on the frontiers. Men who had graduated bottom of their classes, such as the Confederate John Bell Hood, destined in peacetime to become a quartermaster in some quiet backwater, were catapulted into leading whole armies during the war.

The South, despite its strong military traditions, realized that, faced by the Union army and navy, it would be hopelessly outnumbered right from the start. On the other hand, the South was blessed with the boldest

ROBERT EDWARD LEE (1807–1870)

Lee was born in Stratford, Virginia, the son of General Henry Lee. His father died when he was 11 but Lee was determined to follow in his father's footsteps as a soldier. He entered West Point in 1825 and graduated in 1829. By 1834 he had been made a chief engineer and became a first lieutenant two years later, a captain in 1838, and by 1844 was one of the board of visitors at West Point. He was assigned to General Scott's personal staff during the Mexican War and is credited with positioning the American batteries at Vera Cruz and other engagements. Lee was in Washington in October 1859 and was given the responsibility of dealing with John Brown's raiding

party at Harper's Ferry. In March 1861 Lee was offered the command of the Union army but he could not, in his heart, draw his sword against his own state, and resigned his commission in April. Initially he was assigned to Georgia, South Carolina, and Florida. After the Battle of Seven Pines, when General Joseph Johnston was severely wounded, Lee was offered the command of the Army of Northern Virginia and threw himself straight into the new role, fighting the Seven Days' Battles, which effectively stopped McClellan from threatening Richmond. Lee became a hero of the South and was nicknamed "Uncle Robert." He beat the Union army at the Second Bull Run but the volume of casualties and attrition led to a stalemate at Antietam in September 1862. Lee was again successful at Fredericksburg in December and Chancellorsville in April 1863, but made costly mistakes at Gettysburg and again at Malvern Hill, and from mid-1864 was forced to fight a defensive campaign against the overwhelming strength of the Union army under Grant. Lee became Commander-in-Chief in January 1864 and successfully defended Richmond and Petersburg until April 1865, when, cornered and outnumbered, he surrendered his army at Appomattox Courthouse. After the war Lee applied for the post-war amnesty offered to former Confederates who swore to renew their allegiance to the United States. This was never granted, however, because his application was mislaid and was not uncovered until the 1970s. Lee died of heart disease in Lexington in October 1870, something he had been suffering from since 1863.

FORT SUMTER

Fort Sumter is an island fortification located in Charleston, South Carolina. Today it is a National Monment and operated by the National Park Service. The fort was named after General Thomas Sumter, a revolutionary war hero. Construction began in 1829, but was still unfinished in 1861 when the Civil War broke out.

Fort Sumter is most famous for being the site where the first shots of the Civil War were fired. The first battle of Fort Sumter was on April 12, 1861. Commanded by General P.G.T Beauregard, Confederate artillery fired on the Union garrison, with exchange of fire lasting 34 hours. The following day at 2:30pm Major Robert Anderson, garrison commander, surrrendered the fort and was evacuated the next day. Confederate troops then occupied the fort for nearly four years.

The second Battle of Fort Sumter was on September 8, 1863. This was a failed attempt by the Union to re-take the fort. Despite being reduced to rubble the site remained in Confederate hands until it was evacuated as William T. Sherman marched through South Carolina in Feburary 1865.

After the Civil War, Fort Sumter was restored by the U.S. military.

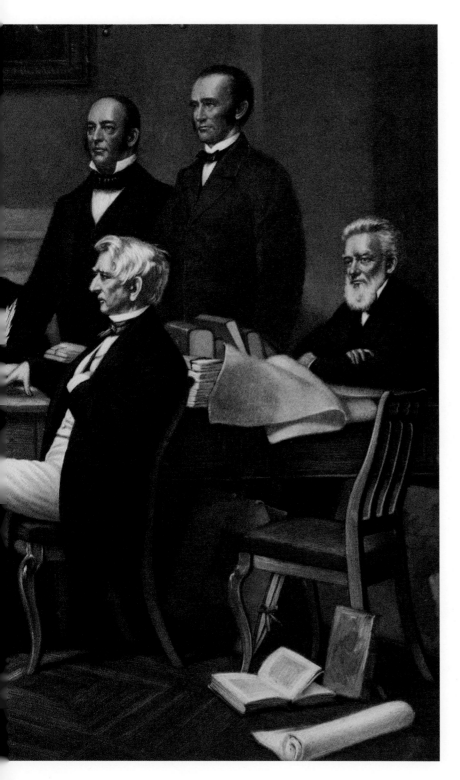

and most competent commanders. Robert E. Lee and Thomas "Stonewall" Jackson led the line, taking the initiative and outwitting Union commanders with far greater forces at their disposal. The South had the unenviable task of defending 4,000 miles (6440km) of front against the **Union** and for the most part chose to do so by taking the offensive and fighting its war in the North's own back yard.

When, eventually, truly competent, visionary, and ruthless commanders emerged from the ranks of the Union army, they were able to wield its immense potential power with some precision. Ulysses S. Grant (a future president), William T. Sherman, and Philip Sheridan were prime examples of such men, determined to achieve ultimate victory and willing to bring total and destructive war to the South.

There were 1,800 or more engagements between the North and South over the four-year period, and half of these would be classed as all-out battles. With a few notable exceptions, the **Confederates** invariably inflicted heavier losses on the North, but manpower was always going to be a problem for the South, in that it

The First Reading of the Emancipation Proclamation before the Cabinet, July 22, 1862. From left to right: Edwin Stanton, Salmon Chase, Lincoln, Gideon Wells, Caleb Smith, William Seward, Montgomery Blair, Edward Bates. *Francis Bicknell Carpenter (1830–1900). Oil on canvas.*

LEFT and OPPOSITE: Civil War battle
re-enactments.

RIGHT: The Gettysburg battlefield. The battle was fought from July 1–3, 1863 in and around the town of Gettysburg, Pennsylvania. The battle involved the largest number of casualties of the entire war.

adamantly refused to officially sanction the recruitment of black soldiers. Despite this, thousands did serve in the ranks of the Confederate armies, and only when it was too late did the South finally concede that it desperately needed black manpower. The North, tentatively at first, recognized the worth of this vast pool of potential soldiers, and against direct orders, black regiments were formed in Kansas and later in the Carolinas. After **Emancipation**, slowly at first but quickly gathering pace, the Union army began to recruit black troops and over 180,000 would later serve, providing the rank and file of over 100 infantry regiments alone.

BELOW: The 27th U.S. Colored Infantry was one of the many black regiments to fight alongside the Army of the Potomac.

RIGHT: White soldiers with a black servant, photographed near Warrenton, Virginia in 1862.

Ultimately, the North was to adopt the so-called Anaconda Strategy – the slow, deliberate strangulation of the South. The blockade and eventual capture of Southern coastal cities and the deep, penetrating, and destructive forays into the heartland of the South began to take effect.

By November 1864 Grant's armies had failed to penetrate Lee's rings of defense around the Confederate capital of Richmond, and it looked as though the war would drag on and that Lincoln would not be re-elected. But complete Southern collapse was closer than the Confederates dared to admit or even the Unionists could have guessed in all their wildest dreams.

The capital finally fell and without it, like many Confederate cities, all hopes for the South lay in ruins. With Union armies converging on the ragtag remnants of his force, Lee had no option but to surrender at Appomattox Courthouse in April 1865, though by then most of the Confederate troops had been imprisoned in Union camps.

The world's largest and most costly civil war had finally come to an end and all that remained of the conflict would be decades of recriminations.

OVERLEAF: Shortly after the Emancipation Proclamation went into effect on January 1, 1863, many freed slaves crossed over to the Union army lines.

OPPOSITE: Maj.Gen. E.O.C. Ord and staff on the south portico of the White House of the Confederacy, 1865.

BELOW: Appomattox Courthouse, Virginia, where General Lee finally surrendered to General Grant in April 1865.

Text-Dependent Questions

1. What side did Ulysses S. Grant fight for during Civil War?

2. What was the so-called Anaconda Strategy?

3. Where is the Appomattox Courthouse?

Research Projects

Explain and summarize the main differences between the Confederacy and the Union.

OPPOSITE: Statue of General "Stonewall" Jackson in Lexington, Virginia.

BELOW: Graves of Confederate soldiers in Hollywood Cemetery marked by wooden boards. Richmond, Virginia, 1865.

Chapter Three
DIXIE, THE OLD SOUTH

The first slaves were brought to Virginia a year before the *Mayflower* arrived in Massachusetts Bay in 1619. However, slavery was already well established in the New World, having been introduced by Portuguese and Spanish colonizers, who used large numbers of the **indigenous** people as slaves.

Large-scale importation of slaves did not begin until the late-17th century, however, and by the time the 13 colonies had risen up in the American Revolution, slavery was permitted by law. After the revolution, the Northern states, principally Delaware, Massachusetts, New York, New Jersey, and Pennsylvania,

gradually ended slavery, but the question arises as to why it persisted in the Southern states, when it had become all but extinct in the North. In Virginia and Maryland the key cash crop had been tobacco, but by the end of the 18th century tobacco was no longer as profitable as it once had been. The replacement crop was cotton, rather than wheat, in that it was more suited to the use of slave labor and rather more profitable than wheat.

New manufacturing processes in England had speeded up and reduced the costs of making cotton thread and textiles, which meant an enormous increase in demand for the raw material. There was a problem in that the type of cotton that could be grown in the American South was not easy to handle, it being difficult to separate the cotton threads from the seeds. Eli Whitney produced a working cotton gin in 1794, solving this problem, and from then on cotton farming spread across the Mississippi, the Appalachian Mountains, and on to Texas, taking slavery with it. Slaves were also used to tend tobacco crops, rice fields and, in Louisiana, sugar canes. By 1830 the South regarded slavery as an economic necessity.

Elsewhere in the New World slavery was dying out, partly due to economics and partly for ethical reasons. Without the American Civil War, nearly 30 years into the future, it

OPPOSITE: African American slave family representing five generations all born on the plantation of J. J. Smith, Beaufort, South Carolina.

RIGHT: Savannah Cotton Exchange, Savannah, Georgia.

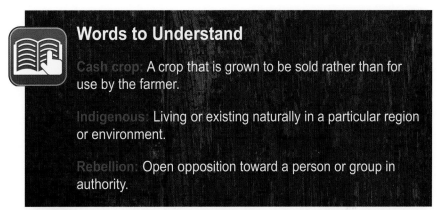

Words to Understand

Cash crop: A crop that is grown to be sold rather than for use by the farmer.

Indigenous: Living or existing naturally in a particular region or environment.

Rebellion: Open opposition toward a person or group in authority.

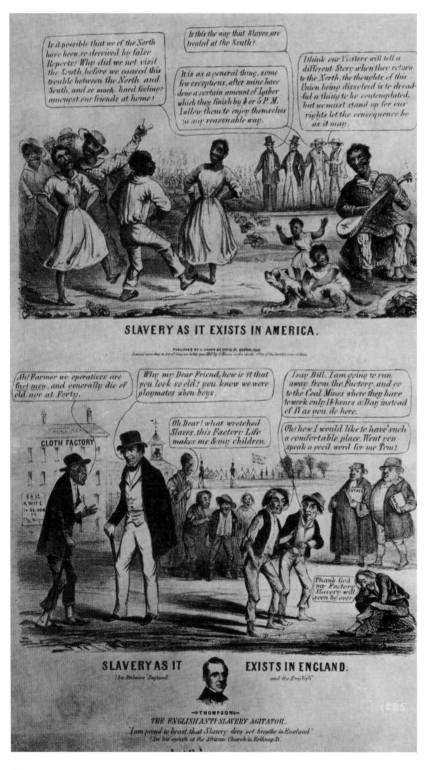

is unlikely that slavery would have died a natural death in the South.

Contrary to most views of the South at this time, the vast majority of whites did not own slaves, and there were only around 25 percent who did or who were linked directly to slave-owning families. By 1850 around half of these owned less than five slaves, and only one percent owned more than 100. At the height of the slave-owning period, only four or five slave-owners owned 1,000 slaves, while an average-sized plantation needed no more than 20 or 30 to work cotton, rice, or sugar crops. Most slaves did not work on plantations; rather they fulfilled the role of hired hands on Southern farms, working alongside their owners in the fields. In larger plantations, and in cities, there were considerable numbers of highly skilled slaves; these built houses, made casks, laid railroads, drove trains, and virtually ran Richmond's tobacco manufacturing industry.

To buy a slave was to make a considerable investment, because once owned, a slave needed to be fed and looked after, even if there was no work. Slave-owners would hire out their slaves, perhaps for $100 a year, having cost the owner between $1,500 and $2,000 to buy. Most of the slaves who constructed the railroads and worked in the tobacco factories in

LEFT: *Slavery as it Exists in America.* A cartoon defending slavery.

OPPOSITE: A Union soldier stands with African Americans on the plantation of Thomas F. Drayton, Hilton Head Island, South Carolina, 1862. Photo by Henry P. Moore, May 1862.

Richmond had been hired out by plantation-owners.

A child born into slavery could be worth as little as $100, but as it reached maturity, its value to the slave-owner would increase. There was a flourishing trade in slaves from Virginia and Maryland, and these were sold to newer states in the Deep South. In fact, after 1808, when further importation of slaves was outlawed, the internal slave trade became a vital

part of the system to provide new slaves where they were needed most. In the vast majority of cases mothers were not subjected to the trauma of having their children torn away from them and sold, they were nearly always sold together. Likewise, couples were rarely separated.

The legal position of slaves was, perhaps, the most confusing aspect of the "peculiar institution," as the Southerners put it. On the one hand

slaves were considered chattels, like a chair or a horse – on the other hand, they had responsibility for their own actions, and could be tried in court for any crime they may have committed. In Georgia, for example, the conviction of a slave for murder was quashed at an appeal court hearing on the grounds that the owner had not paid for a defense attorney for his slave.

It is clear that slaves were recognized as human beings in

ABOVE: An engraving depicting African American slaves working on a cotton plantation. Matt Morgan, 1887.

Southern law. In Mississippi in 1821, a white man murdered a slave and his defense was based on the assumption that killing a slave could not be murder. The white judge was having none of this and told the defendant: "[The slave] is still a human being and possesses all those rights, of which he is not deprived by the positive provisions of the law. By the provisions of our law, a slave may commit murder, and be punished by death. Is not the slave a reasonable creature, is he not a human being, [and since] even the killing of a lunatic, an idiot or even a child unborn, is murder, as much as the killing of a philosopher, has not the slave as much reason as a lunatic, an idiot, or an unborn child?"

The judge thought the answer was yes and sentenced the murderer to death.

The South wrestled with the paradox of owning another human being, while creating laws to protect the enslaved. Legal protection grew, not least in the case of proving actual ownership, the law presuming that a black person was a slave unless they had documents to prove to the contrary. In practice, this meant that unscrupulous individuals could make forays into non-slave states, snatch black people and present them as slaves in the South. By 1850 the slave population stood at 3.2 million. Each year, however, thousands were freed, many of mixed race, being the offspring of slaves and their former masters.

Slaves could also use the law to obtain their freedom, and could purchase themselves if they were able to save enough money. Usually, when this happened, the former slave was required to leave the state, there being no wish to have large numbers of freed slaves on the loose, that could band together and engineer a revolt. Only six percent of the black population of the South were freed men and even they were held in comparative poverty by a restrictive mix of custom and law.

By 1860 there were 4 million slaves in the South and just 250,000 freed men. In practice, while laws existed to protect slaves from being punished too harshly by their masters, there was no one to actually police the law. Conditions were therefore variable: wealthier plantation owners were able to provide more stable, fairer environments, compared with less established owners, who worked their slaves harder and kept them in worse conditions.

Divisions existed even among the slaves themselves: field hands would work up to or in excess of 12 hours each day, allowed perhaps a half-day on a Saturday and a full day's rest on Sunday. House slaves, on the other hand, were regarded almost as one of the owner's family and enjoyed better living conditions as a result.

Force was at the heart of the system, however, the most common punishment being the whip, wielded by either a black driver or a white overseer. Whippings typically consisted of 20 or 30 lashes, with 50 or so for more serious misdemeanors. Punishment was carried out in public as an warning to the other slaves.

BELOW: Woodcut depicting the revolt of Nat Turner, an American slave and leader of an 1831 rebellion of slaves in Southampton County, Virginia.

RIGHT: Preserved plantation slave
homes in Charleston, South Carolina.

On rare occasions, resentment over the treatment of slaves would boil over into open revolt. In 1831, Nat Turner, a slave owned by a wealthy Virginian farmer, Joseph Travis, lead what became known as Nat Turner's Rebellion. Over the space of three months, never involving more than around 60 or so armed men, Turner was able to kill 55 whites, though in the end he was cornered and captured, and Turner and 17 of his followers were hanged. In a white backlash against the slaves, up to 200 lost their lives, but the "**rebellion**" had terrified the white population and rumors spread of even larger uprisings across the South.

BELOW: Discovery of Nat Turner by Benjamin Phipps on October 30, 1831. *Engraving by William Henry Shelton (1840–1890).*

Witney's invention meant that upland short cotton could be made into a more lucrative crop. However, the unfortunate effect of this was that it strengthend the economic requirement for slavery in the United States.

Before the cotton gin was invented, the seeds from the cotton plant had to be removed by hand, a process that had been time-consuming and labor-intensive. The word "gin" derived from the shortened word "engine." Whitney's patented, mechanical device worked liked a strainer or sieve. The cotton would be run through a wooden drum and a series of hooks would then pull the cotton fibers through a mesh. The seeds would not fit through the mesh and would fall to the outside.

It has been reported that Whitney told a story wherein he was pondering an improved method of seeding the cotton when he was inspired by observing a cat attempting to pull a chicken through a fence. It was only the feathers that would be allowed through.

A single cotton gin could generate up to 55 pounds (25kg) of cleaned cotton daily. This in turn, contributed to the economic development of the Southern states, as planters earned great profits, promoting them to grow increasingly more cotton crops. As slavery was the cheapest form of labor the farmers would simply purchase more slaves.

Whitney received a patent for his cotton gin invention in 1794, but it was not validated until 1807. Whitney and his partner, Miller, did not intend to sell the gins. Rather, they expected to charge farmers for cleaning their cotton – two-fifths of the value, paid in cotton. This scheme was ultimately resented by the farmers and with the mechanical simplicity of the device and the primitive state of patent law, made infringement inevitable, so gins from other makers found ready sales. In the end, patent infringement lawsuits consumed the profits and their cotton gin company went out of business in 1797. In 1817, Whitney married Henrietta Edwards. They went on to have four children. Whitney died on January 8, 1825 at 59 years old.

ELI WHITNEY (1765–1825)

Eli Whitney, the famous American inventor is best known for inventing the cotton gin. It was one of the key inventions of the industrial revolution. Before the Civil War the cotton gin was responsible for shaping the economy of the South.

There had been other such attempts earlier in the 19th century, notably by Gabriel Prosser in 1800 and Denmark Vessy in 1822, but neither turned into actual revolts. These were rare, as had been the case at the height of the Roman Empire, but when the Union troops flooded into the Southern states during the American Civil War, such was the reaction from freed slaves that 180,000 or more donned the blue of the Union to fight against their former masters.

The South was not full of aristocrats as Hollywood would have us believe, and the vast majority of white farmers did not own slaves. They farmed at subsistence levels, unable to

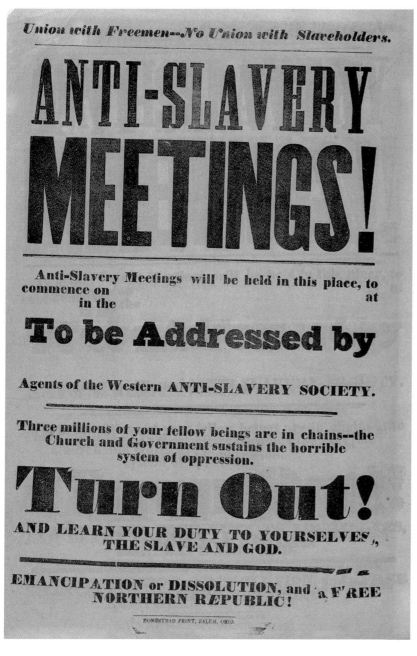

Union with Freemen--No Union with Slaveholders.

ANTI-SLAVERY MEETINGS!

Anti-Slavery Meetings will be held in this place, to commence on
in the   at

To be Addressed by

Agents of the Western ANTI-SLAVERY SOCIETY.

Three millions of your fellow beings are in chains--the Church and Government sustains the horrible system of oppression.

Turn Out!

AND LEARN YOUR DUTY TO YOURSELVES, THE SLAVE AND GOD.

EMANCIPATION or DISSOLUTION, and a FREE NORTHERN REPUBLIC!

HOMESTEAD PRINT, SALEM, OHIO.

crops were more common in the Northern states. New Orleans was central to the trade between North and South and there was a mutual dependency, which for some time had cemented the states together as a Union.

Gradually, over the years, the South began to set itself apart from the Northern states, and its importance as a producer of cotton, with its attendant reliance on slavery, was to encourage this feeling of superiority. In 1800 the United States exported 40 percent of its entire crop of 200,000 bales of cotton, with production reaching 2 million bales each year by the end of the 1830s. Two decades later and this had increased to 3 million bales and it had reached almost 5 million by the beginning of the American Civil War.

Farms in Tennessee, Kentucky, Maryland, and North Carolina grew tobacco, and the low-lying regions of Georgia and South Carolina rice, but cotton was king. The cotton would be planted in the spring and early summer, and would be harvested in the fall and early winter, when towns and cities would be filled to bursting with bales of cotton, waiting to begin their long journey to eventual markets, either in the North or in Europe.

By this time, both North and South were losing population to the West, as day after day more virgin territory was being opened up and the Native Americans were being driven from their traditional lands.

LEFT: An anti-slavery poster from 1850.

OPPOSITE: A Methodist anti-slavery meeting.

afford the investment in slaves needed to grow more lucrative crops. The basic foodstuffs were corn, sweet potatoes, peas, and beans, supplemented by chickens and eggs, while game and fish could be had for free. Above all, they were fiercely independent and suspicious of outsiders.

While rice, tobacco, cotton, and sugar were the main cash crops in the Deep South, wheat and other cereal

This drain would soon contribute to the further stagnation of the South's economy.

The simple fact was that subsistence farmers, though not exactly poor, did not produce enough to sell on the open market, which meant that the towns and cities were underdeveloped, being merely service centers for the **cash crops** of cotton and tobacco. Slavery added to the problem: slaves produced cash-generating crops, but the money went to their owners. The South could feed itself, but do little else.

In the North, meanwhile, in the two decades preceding the Civil War, rapid changes were afoot that would see an enormous gulf widen between North and South. In New York, New Jersey, Pennsylvania, and New England, factories and mills were springing up, and manufacturing was developing even in the agricultural Midwest. But as for the South, the industrial revolution sweeping the United States had virtually passed it by. Apart from a few cotton mills and simple processing facilities for flour, tobacco, and wood, the South was falling behind, and it would remain a predominantly agricultural economy.

By 1860 some 85 percent of the South's workforce labored in the fields, compared with only 40 percent in the North and West. Only ten per cent of the population in the South lived in large towns or cities, compared with over 25 percent elsewhere. Southern towns were tiny by Northern standards, being virtually dead except at harvest time, when they temporarily sprang to life. Moreover, the South, being predominantly agricultural, had to buy its manufactured goods either from the North or from Europe.

There were some Southerners who could see the danger of allowing the North not only to be the manufacturing base of the country, but also the principal point of entry for goods from abroad. But the wealth of the South lay in the hands of a few: these few large plantation owners had everything to lose and nothing to gain from a change in the status quo.

ABOVE: The Abolition of the Slave Trade.
Cartoon of 1792 by Isaac Cruikshank, depicting the inhumanity of the slave trade. It shows Captain John Kimber, of Bristol, England, ill-treating a young black girl of 15.

OPPOSITE: Old slave cabins at the Kingsley Plantation in the Timucuan Ecological and Historic National Preserve. Jacksonville, Florida.

These wealthy planters felt that industry, if it came to the South, would create a new wealthy class that would challenge their power. They continued to reinvest their surplus cash into more land and slaves, while the transport infrastructure, though adequate to deal with crops, could not compete with that of the North. Labor was also seen as a potential problem: to get subsistence farmers to work in industry they would have to be paid high wages, the alternative being slaves, who were expensive to buy and needed a higher initial investment. They realized that industry would attract cheap immigrant labor and that if they allowed slaves to be hired out to the manufacturers they would lack the overall control they had previously enjoyed. As a representative of the planters, John Hammand remarked: "Whenever a slave is made a mechanic he is more than half freed, and soon becomes, as we too well know, and all history attests, with rare exceptions, the most corrupt and turbulent of his class."

The South may not have liked it, and may even have denied it, but it realized it was reliant on the North and on Europe. Nevertheless, the land provided the common farmer with sufficient food to feed his family and provided a handsome profit for the large land-owning, slave-holding class. Unlike most of the rest of the United States, the South chose to stay comparatively unchanging and unchanged.

It was clear to new immigrants to the United States that the South had

little to offer in the way of opportunity, so they gravitated to the North and West. This was another loss to the South; as enormous opportunities for progress passed it by, so the rigid caste system bound it to the past.

The Southern white population, in what was in reality a backward and rural society, had learned how to be self-reliant, though it had not developed beyond the basic requirements of frontier life. The South was immersed in violence, the inherent violence of slavery, with a white population that feared its own downfall if it were ever to lose control over its slaves. In other words, the end of slavery would ultimately make it subordinate to an "inferior race." Abolitionists, therefore, represented the enemy, intent on exposing the South to murderous mobs of freed blacks. They had to be stopped, whatever the means, otherwise the survival of the South lay in the balance.

Violence was endemic. A gentleman would duel with an adversary, horsewhip an inferior and would fight, no holds barred, until one of them was reduced to a bloody pulp. Southerners had the reputation of being good officers and equally good soldiers, and individual

ABOVE: A cotton press producing cotton bales in operation in the South after the Civil War. The machine had a large vertical screw turned by horses or mules harnessed to long poles. ca. 1875.

OPPOSITE: Constructed in 1869, The 7th Regiment Memorial honors the 58 men who died defending the Union during the Civil War. The bronze statue by American sculptor John Quincy Adams Ward depicts a soldier with his rifle. New York City, New York.

Research Projects

Explain why slavery persisted in Southern states long after many Northern states, principally Delaware, Massachusetts, New York, New Jersey, and Pennsylvania gradually ended it.

ABOVE: Slaves sitting near their cabins on a Port Royal, South Carolina plantation after the arrival of Union forces in late 1861.

OPPOSITE: A newly freed African American group of men and a few children posing by a canal against the ruins of Richmond, Virginia. Photo made after Richmond was taken by Union troops on April 3, 1865.

Text-Dependent Questions

1. Who were the first to bring slavery to the Americas?

2. Who was Nat Turner?

3. List four cash crops produced in the South.

military skills were highly regarded. In a sparsely populated rural environment it was not the done thing to have a formal education: in 1850 illiteracy stood at 20 percent, compared with less than half a percent in New England.

The wealthy provided private tutors for their children and further education for boys was at the military academies. Northern teachers and Northern literature were considered to be subversive.

Gradually, over the decades, Southern nationalism began to gain momentum in the slave-owning states. Some based their views on the argument that slavery freed white men from manual and boring duties, postulating that all whites in a slave state were aristocrats and needed to be served. They looked at the turmoil and chaos in the North and saw the South as a haven of peace and tranquillity. Above all, the "aristocratic" Southerners, who held the bulk of the land and made their profits from slavery, saw their class as a noble elite. They were self-made men, and had a right to their position in society through their ownership of land and slaves.

Others even held the view that Northern industrialists were more immoral than the slave-owners of the South, in that they paid low wages while keeping most of the profits for themselves. The Southerner, on the other hand, obviously took less of the profits, in that he looked after his slaves and ensured they wanted for nothing.

Thus the South developed its own distinctive spin on life; it now sought independence in the belief that its society was superior to that of the North – unique, distinctive and worth fighting for. The North, it believed, was bent on destroying the South and all it stood for, therefore abolitionists, Northern politicians and even the Northern population at large were the sworn enemies of the South.

As events lurched towards the year 1861 and the outbreak of civil war, the South would be expected to prove more than its nationalistic aspirations; it would have to prove its military supremacy to gain the status it so earnestly desired.

RIGHT: Ex-slaves hiding in the swamps of Louisiana. Some African American men chose exile in the wilderness or Indian territories. 1873. *19th century engraving with modern color.*

TIME LINE OF THE CIVIL WAR

1860

November 6
Abraham Lincoln elected president.

December 20
South Carolina secedes from the Union, followed two months later by other states.

1861

February 9
Jefferson Davis becomes the first and only President of the Confederate States of America.

March 4
Lincoln sworn in as 16th President of the United States.

April 12
Confederates, under Beauregard, open fire on Fort Sumter at Charleston, South Carolina.

April 15
Lincoln issues a proclamation calling for 75,000 volunteers.

April 17
Virginia secedes from the Union, followed by three other states, making an 11-state Confederacy.

April 19
Blockade proclamation issued by Lincoln.

April 20
Robert E. Lee resigns his command in the United States Army.

July 4
Congress authorizes a call for half a million volunteers.

July 21
Union forces, under McDowell, defeated at Bull Run.

July 27
McClellan replaces McDowell.

November 1
McClellan becomes general-in-chief of Union forces after the resignation of Winfield Scott.

November 8
Two Confederate officials are seized en route to Great Britain by the Union navy.

1862

February 6
Grant captures Fort Henry in Tennessee.

March 8–9
The Confederate ironclad *Merrimac* sinks two Union warships, then fights the *Monitor*.

April 6–7
Confederates attack Grant at Shiloh on the Tennessee river.

April 24
Union ships under Farragut take New Orleans.

May 31
Battle of Seven Pines, where Joseph E. Johnston is badly wounded when he nearly defeats McClellan's army.

June 1
Robert E. Lee takes over from Johnston and renames the force the Army of Northern Virginia.

June 25–July 1
Lee attacks McClellan near Richmond during the Seven Days' Battles. McClellan retreats towards Washington.

July 11
Henry Halleck becomes general -in-chief of the Union army.

August 29–30
Union army, under Pope, defeated by Jackson and Longstreet at the Second Battle of Bull Run.

September 4–9
Lee invades the North, pursued by McClellan's Union army.

September 17
Battle of Antietam. Both sides are badly mauled. Lee withdraws to Virginia.

September 22
Preliminary Emancipation Proclamation issued by Lincoln.

November 7
McClellan replaced by Burnside as commander of the Army of the Potomac.

December 13
Burnside decisively defeated at Fredericksburg, Virginia, 1863.

1863
January 1
Lincoln issues the final Emancipation Proclamation.

January 29
Grant assumes command of the Army of the West.

March 3
U.S. Congress authorizes conscription.

May 1–4
Hooker is decisively defeated by Lee at the Battle of Chancellorsville. Stonewall Jackson is mortally wounded.

June 3
Lee invades the North, heading into Pennsylvania.

June 28
George Meade replaces Hooker as commander of the Army of the Potomac.

July 1–3
Lee is defeated at the Battle of Gettysburg.

July 4
Vicksburg – the last Confederate stronghold on the Mississippi – falls to Grant and the Confederacy is now split in two.

July 13–16
Draft riots in New York

July 18
54th Massachusetts, under Shaw, fails in its assault against Fort Wagner, South Carolina.

August 21
Quantrill's raiders murder the inhabitants of Lawrence, Kansas

September 19–20
Bragg's Confederate Army of Tennessee defeats General Rosecrans at Chickamauga.

October 16
Grant given command of all operations in the West.

November 19
Lincoln gives his famous Gettysburg Address.

November 23–25
Grant defeats Bragg at Chattanooga.

1864
March 9
Grant assumes command of all armies of the Union. Sherman takes Grant's old job as commander in the West.

May 5–6
Battle of the Wilderness.

May 8–12
Battle of Spotsylvania.

June 1–3
Battle of Cold Harbor.

June 15
Union troops miss a chance to capture Petersburg.

July 20
Sherman defeats Hood at Atlanta.

August 29
Former General McClellan becomes the Democratic nominee for president.

September 2
Atlanta is captured by Sherman.

October 19
Sheridan defeats Early's Confederates in the Shenandoah Valley.

November 8
Lincoln is re-elected president.

November 15
Sherman begins his March to the Sea.

December 15–16
Hood is defeated at the Battle of Nashville.

December 21 Sherman reached Savannah in Georgia.

1865
January 31
Thirteenth amendment approved to abolish slavery.

February 3
Peace conference between Lincoln and Confederate vice president fails at Hampton Roads, Virginia.

March 4
Lincoln inaugurated as president.

March 25
Lee's last offensive is defeated after four hours at Petersburg

April 2
Grant pushes through Lee's defensive lines at Petersburg. Richmond is evacuated as Union troops enter.

April 4
Lincoln tours Richmond.

April 9
Lee surrenders his army to Grant at Appomattox Courthouse, Virginia.

April 10
Major victory celebrations in Washington.

April 14
Lincoln shot in a Washington theater.

April 15
Lincoln dies and Andrew Johnson becomes president.

April 18
Confederate General Johnston surrenders to Sherman in North Carolina.

April 19
Lincoln's funeral procession.

April 26
Lincoln's assassin, Booth, is shot and dies in Virginia

May 23–24
Victory parade held in Washington

December 6
Thirteenth Amendment approved by Congress. It is ratified and slavery is formally abolished

BELOW: The Appomattox County Confederate Memorial stands on the grounds of the Appomattox County Courthouse, Virginia. This memorial was erected by the sons of Confederate veterans.

Educational Videos about the American Civil War

The Gettysburg Address
A speech by U.S. President Abraham Lincoln, one of the best-known in American history. It was delivered by Lincoln during the American Civil War, on the afternoon of Thursday, November 19, 1863, at the dedication of the Soldiers' National Cemetery in Gettysburg, Pennsylvania.

Everyday Animated Map
A useful video explaining how the Union and Confederate armies gained ground through the various battles.

"Dear Sarah," A Soldier's Farewell to his Wife
A Civil War soldier's heartbreaking farewell letter written before his death at Bull Run.

The War Between the States
Historian Garry Adleman gives an overview of the causes, campaigns, and conclusion of the Civil War.

History, Key Figures, and Battles
A useful, concise dramatized, video explaining the American Civil War.

EXAMPLES OF CONFEDERATE UNIFORMS

Robert E. Lee in his general's uniform

Trooper, Stuart's Cavalry Corps.

Infantry Soldier

Marines

Virginia Cavalry

Louisiana
Tigers

Georgia
Infantry

4th Alabama
Regiment

South
Carolina
Regiment

Engineer

EXAMPLES OF UNION (FEDERAL) UNIFORMS

Ulysses S. Grant in his general's uniform

Indiana Regiment

5th New York Volunteers

39th New York Voluntry Infantry Regiment

Iron Brigade of the U.S.

U.S. Marine Corps

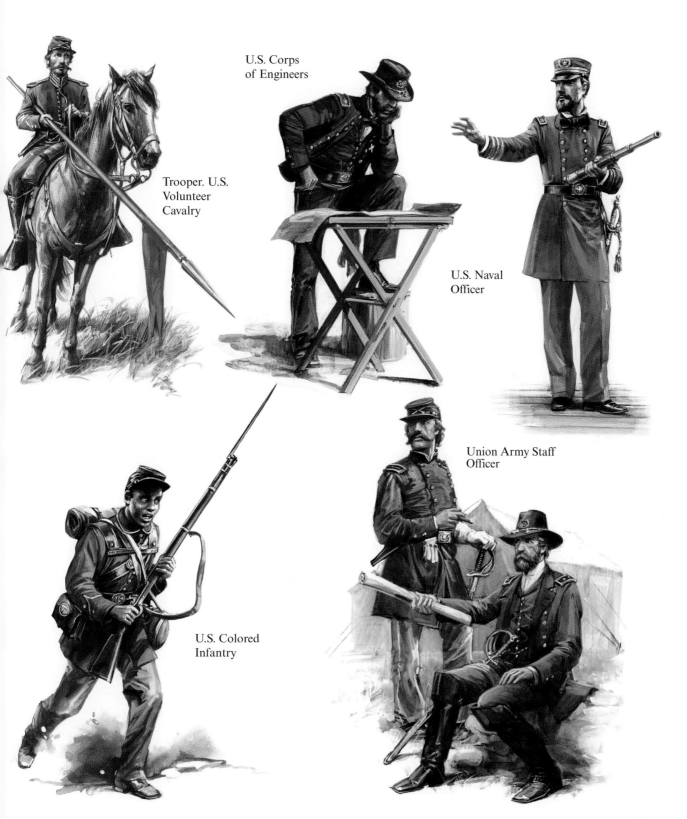

U.S. Corps
of Engineers

Trooper. U.S.
Volunteer
Cavalry

U.S. Naval
Officer

Union Army Staff
Officer

U.S. Colored
Infantry

Series Glossary of Key Terms

Abolitionist A person who wants to eliminate slavery.

Antebellum A term describing the United States before the Civil War.

Artillery Large bore firearms like cannons and mortars.

Assassination A murder for political reasons (usually an important person).

Cash Crop A crop such as cotton, sugar cane, or tobacco sold for cash.

Cavalry A section of the military mounted on horseback.

Confederacy Also called the South or the Confederate States of America. A term given to 11 southern states seceding from the United States in 1860 and 1861.

Copperhead A person in the North who sympathized with the South during the Civil War.

Dixie A nickname given to states in the south-east United States.

Dred Scott Decision A decision made by the Supreme Court that said Congress could not outlaw slavery.

Emancipation An act of setting someone free from slavery.

Gabion A basket filled with rocks and earth used to build fortifications.

Fugitive Slave Law A law passed by Congress in 1850 that stipulated escaped slaves in free states had to be retured to their owners.

Infantry Soldiers that travel and fight on foot.

North The states located in the north of the United States, also called the Union.

Plantation An area of land especially in hot parts of the world where crops such as cotton and tobacco are grown.

Slavery The state of a person who is owned or under the control of another.

Secession Withdrawal from the Federal goverment of the United States.

Sectionalism A tendency to be concerned with local interests and customs ahead of the larger country.

South The states located in the south of the United States, also called the Confederacy.

Union The name given to the states that stayed loyal to the United States.

West Point The United States Military Academy.

Yankee A nickname given for people from the North and Union soldiers.

Further Reading and Internet Resources

WEBSITES

http://www.civilwar.org

http://www.historyplace.com/civilwar

http://www.historynet.com/civil-war

www.britannica.com/event/American-Civil-War

BOOKS

Bruce Catton. *The Centennial History of the Civil War,* Doubleday, 1962. Kindle edition 2013.

Ulysses S. Grant. *The Complete Personal Memoirs of Ulysses S*. Grant Seven Treasures Publications, 2009

James Robertson and Neil Kagan. *The Untold Civil War: Exploring the Human Side of War*. National Geographic, 2011.

If you enjoyed this book take a look at Mason Crest's other war series:

The Vietnam War, World War II, Major U.S. Historical Wars.

Index

In this book, page numbers in **_bold italic font_** indicate photos or videos.

PHOTOGRAPHIC ACKNOWLEDGEMENTS
All images in this book are supplied by the
Library of Congess/public domain and under license
from © Shutterstock.com other than the following:
Regency House Publishing Limited: 7, 72-73, 74-75.

The content of this book was first published as
CIVIL WAR.

ABOUT THE AUTHOR
Johnathan Sutherland & Diane Canwell
Together, Diane Canwell and Jonathan Sutherland are
the authors of 150 books, and have written
extensively about the American Civil War. Both
have a particular interest in American history, and its
military aspects in particular. Several of their books
have attracted prizes and awards, including New York
Library's Best of Reference and Book List's
Editor's Choice.